THE
Secular Case
FOR
Religion

PHIL DOVE

WESTBOW
PRESS®
A DIVISION OF THOMAS NELSON
& ZONDERVAN

WestBow Press books may be ordered through booksellers or by contacting:

WestBow Press
A Division of Thomas Nelson & Zondervan
1663 Liberty Drive
Bloomington, IN 47403
www.westbowpress.com
844-714-3454

ISBN: 978-1-6642-3295-2 (sc)
ISBN: 978-1-6642-3296-9 (e)

Library of Congress Control Number: 2021908766

Print information available on the last page.

WestBow Press rev. date: 05/10/2021

Contents

Preface

I owe the idea for this book to friends with whom I often disagree when we discuss things such as politics, religion or our respective world views. Some of these friends are among my closest and dearest, in part because our bond is strong enough that we can disagree but do so constructively and without it being personal-it's about ideas and not about personal distaste for one another.

I like to think that I have a reason for the things that I believe and the principles that I hold. Having people who hold different views and challenge me on my own views, forces me to think. They push me to re-examine the reason for my own views and either confirm that there are good reasons for what I believe or cause me to change my mind through their reasoning.

In one of those conversations, a friend and I were talking about government social programs and the perception among some, that those who oppose more money for 'safety net programs' such as welfare, food stamps and public housing are just greedy and uncaring. The conversation went to a discussion about the role and effectiveness of government and the role of personal giving to charity. During that discussion, we couldn't help but reference a famous and comprehensive study done some years ago by Pew Research on charitable giving patterns in the United States. The findings, which I'll touch on more later, were sometimes counterintuitive and had several things that were thought provoking. Among them, when combined with what we know about political sentiment in areas of the country, showed that charitable giving was almost uniformly higher in places where governmental social programs were not as popular. In other words, if we make a very general assumption that charities serve those less fortunate, it appeared that there was a strong sentiment not on whether to help others but whether that should be done by the government or by individuals making individual choices. I must admit that my bias leaned in that latter direction, as well, even though some friends found it difficult to understand that thinking.

My friend pointed out that the high levels of charitable giving were also in areas that were traditionally very religious. He argued, probably correctly, that much of that charitable giving went to churches or other religious organizations. He didn't say it directly, but implicit in what he said was that giving to religious organizations was somewhat less valid, less giving or less compassionate. Not being very religious himself, he seemed to imply, or at least I read into the response, that you should take out religious giving as a 'charity' because money given there went to promote that religion. Hence, if you backed out the giving to religious causes that the picture would be different.

He was challenging me and what I thought with his words. I was forced to think about what he said and that thought process was the genesis for this book.

What follows is the result of that thinking. It's not an

academic work, heavily footnoted with research studies on my perspectives. It is, however, deeply introspective and a look at, in a sense, 'what good is religion?'

Nor is this work an attempt to bring a religious conversion. What it is, is an effort to show the value of religion to society--to the people who make up the citizenry--totally apart from any religious belief or practice or even a belief in an afterlife at all. It is, quite simply, a totally secular case for the positive effect that religion has on society in the United States.

Having said that, I will add one caveat and that being that the 'look' will be from a Christian and, to a lesser degree, a Judeo perspective and also primarily from the perspective of someone living in the United States, as the author does. I fully realize that is a subset of religion, albeit in the United States the largest subset. However, this is the perspective that the largest portion of readers will understand and can relate to, which is the goal even though it does result in a higher-level view that is not necessarily a global one, either geographically or contextually.

It is probably stating the obvious to say that the main purpose of religious organizations, very generally speaking, is to promote their religious beliefs in some form or another, either in overtly religious contexts such as church services and education, or in ministering in ways that they think evidence their beliefs about helping others. We can admit that, and most people can even be fine with that. A religion is about the eternal, things not only of this world but of things to come. If you really believe that you know the way to Heaven and eternal life or peace, then it would be the height of an uncaring and self-centered attitude not to share that with others. So at least in that way it is true, though a cynical way to say it, that the primary purpose of religion is to promote religion. Another way to say it is that people with strong religious beliefs desire to share their good fortune with others, both the eternal and the temporal. To people of deep principle, the eternal and the temporal are not two separate things but two sides of the same coin and they try to live their lives to reflect that.

Yet, upon examination, we find that religion does much more than just seek to promote its view of the eternal, the way to Heaven or, if you are more cynical, the way to perpetuate itself. Evidence, both data-driven and anecdotal, shows that there are tangible benefits for society. Even aside from a belief that there is more to life than what we find in a sometimes unfair and ugly world, we can see that people of faith, and faith-based organizations, are an asset to a community and to society, as a whole.

Even if you are not religious or don't have a belief in God (or 'a god'), then I think we will find that you still benefit from religion and that there is still good that comes from religion. At the highest level, religion provides a certain basis for belief, a 'worldview' if you will. For people to whom religion is a part of their personal make-up, this provides a moral compass and cultural context that guides, at least in general terms, how they act and view the world. Though this moral view isn't the main purpose of our discussion, it is not something that should be discounted. People who try to live their religious beliefs, by definition, try to live by the moral teachings that those beliefs espouse. A person of faith will not live by a relativist view of morality where 'everyone does what is right in their own eyes' but, as best they can, will try to live by the principles that align with their faith and its teachings.

Even if an atheist or skeptic doesn't believe that you will face divine punishment for stealing or killing, it's still a very good thing to live around a person who doesn't steal or kill because they do believe they will be divinely held accountable. The bottom line is, whether you agree or disagree with their reason, it's good to live around people who believe and live like that. Ok, so that's a dramatic example but that doesn't make it any less true. Even if you aren't kind to your neighbor and welcome someone who just moved in next door because you think it's a moral imperative, you still get a benefit from a person who is kind and helpful because they are trying to live out the teaching to love your neighbor from their church or synagogue.

Of course, there are exceptions and part of most religious belief systems is a view that humans are imperfect, at the least, and we can certainly admit that religious people do not always live out their beliefs or, to use a cliché, 'practice what they preach'. But the reverse is also true: that a person of faith, who holds deeply to the precepts of that faith, tries to live in a way that their faith teaches and to live in a way that reflects, in practice, the tenets of their theology. Though that person may not do so all the time, or even as often as they should, they hopefully try to do better. That effort will then be reflected in how they interact with those they come in contact with throughout their days. And the more they try to do that, the more positive impact they have on the community around them.

Moving away from the thought of religion as a moral compass and back to the original discussion with my good friend, religious belief also guides a view of helping others. That includes giving to religious-based charities, because religious-based charities are not solely devoted to religious study but serve the communities around them in a tremendously broad range of ways. Every religion talks about how we relate to our fellow man and to the world around us. In Christianity this is found, for example, in the parable of the Good Samaritan and Jesus' teaching to love your neighbor. It is this fundamental premise that is the point of this writing. Money given to churches and religious charities flows through to the rest of society and the community in ways that are not strictly religious, and in ways that fill gaps and needs that otherwise would go unmet. Even for those that may not be religious, the examples that are shared in the following pages will illustrate that there is a tangible value of religion in society. Even for a person, or a society, that does not subscribe to a religious belief or does so in nothing other than general terms, there is good that comes from religion in America. There is a secular case for religion.

One

Introduction

Someone has said that those who have accomplished most in this life are those that have been most concerned about the next.

Stop and think about that for a minute. That's a profound statement at its heart. The statement says that people whose thoughts are mostly on the spiritual, on the eternal, are most often the ones that have had the most impact on the day to day and the now.

In lots of ways that most of us don't see, there are people of faith who work every day to work towards eternity, while doing so in tangible ways in this life. As is the case with a lot of things, many of us rarely know all that goes on around us unless it affects us or we come in contact with it personally. Yet, every day there are people who serve and help others with little recognition but they are helping to make the world around them better in small ways and large.

However, if we do stop to think about that, all of us actually could think of all sorts of anecdotes that show us how that has been the case. Obviously, deeply religious people give back in the context of the spiritual, their eternal destiny, which is certainly important. A person of faith, who believes in Heaven and believes they know how we, as humans, can get to Heaven wants to share that. Yet part of that eternal view, that we are all made in God's image and all people have inherent value, also motivates people who live their faith with a desire to share with others a helping hand. A way of practicing their faith and showing the inherent value of each person is to help to make the lives of people around them better, and in its simplest form, that is how people with a concern for eternity make a difference in people's lives and in their communities every day.

To follow this line of thinking at the big picture level, each of us could think of examples that we know of or have maybe benefited from. I'm sure that we all are familiar with at least some examples.

One obvious and well known example in our lifetime is that of Mother Teresa, if nothing else because of the awarding of a Nobel Prize. Mother Teresa moved to India after growing up in Europe and spent most of her adult life working in the slums of Calcutta. Among other things, she established a home for those dying of leprosy, AIDs and tuberculosis, an orphanage, a hospital and, in the highly regimented caste society of India, a place for the outcasts and lowest members of society to go. Even if, in some cases, that was simply a place to go in order to have a roof and food to eat and a place to die with dignity. She worked among the most downtrodden, the poorest of the poor, in a place where standards of living, even in good circumstances, were already much lower than where she had grown up. She considered it an act of faith to care for and love those who may have lived in conditions most of us could only imagine, and in that way and in many cases at the end of life to give them a beautiful death worthy of someone created in the image of God.

Though certainly not an isolated case, the case of Mother Teresa is illustrative of the point to be made. First and foremost, she was a devoted adherent to her religious beliefs. She began her study and work in Europe. She became a teacher in Catholic schools prior to her work among the poor. Throughout her life, her primary goal was to tell others about her beliefs in the eternal and she never wavered in that. Indeed, she received a good deal of criticism in certain quarters later in life because of her ongoing advocacy of certain religious beliefs of her church, which she continued to espouse.

Yet in doing so, she lived out her beliefs in a very tangible and earthly way. At the same time she shared her spiritual beliefs, she also lived them in how she ministered to others. A simple act of moving to India, a country with a much lower standard of living and far fewer creature comforts was the first act of sacrifice. Once there, she lived to serve and worked to recruit and equip others to do the same and did so with a conviction that was recognized worldwide when she was awarded the Nobel Peace Prize in 1979.

The award of the Nobel Prize was obviously not for her religious practice and devotion. It was for her relief work in the slums and among the poor of Calcutta. Yet, in reality, it was a recognition of the secular, earthly impact of her spiritual and religious beliefs. It was an acknowledgement of how she put her faith into practice by helping to make the world around her in Calcutta a better place. It was a reward for her life that took her from an early life in Europe to one primarily devoted to serving the downtrodden in

India's second largest city, a city teeming with poverty and homelessness. And while that Nobel Prize was awarded several decades ago now, her legacy still serves others. The religious order she founded in 1950, the Missionaries of Charity, still runs facilities in Calcutta and are still growing in their reach. Even last year, I know of a young man who traveled to India and during his time there, spent time working at the hospital started by Mother Teresa, though she has long since died.

Mother Teresa's case is one of the most well-known because of her receipt of the Nobel Prize but it is certainly not rare. I know personally of several, similar cases. For example, I know doctors who have left a potential lucrative career in the US and are now working in the country of Togo, in Africa, at a hospital founded by a Baptist Christian organization. The hospital, one of the few in the whole country, is critical enough to those underserved people that senior officials of the Togo government were at the most recent groundbreaking of an expansion of the facility. Yet the clinicians and medical staff there serve as volunteers at a compensation fractions of what they could earn if they had stayed in the countries where they received their medical training.

As we will see below, there are religious organizations and people who serve across the globe in ways that provide help to people in need, and provide a tangible value to society and the culture around them. In the discussion to follow, we will see how religion serves others by giving monetarily and then also of time and abilities. We will see how society benefits from religion, even those within society who find no value in religion itself.

We will show that there is a secular case for religion.

Two

Charitable Giving

There was a detailed study by Pew Research some years ago on charitable giving. It looked at charitable giving and how much we, in the United States, gave as individuals to private charities. It went further and matched income to giving patterns, breaking down giving in dollar terms and also as a percentage of income and it included information on where the charitable giving went and to what types of charities.

It also took a detailed look at who gave money to charity, breaking down the giving patterns along several demographics, such as where they live, income levels and how they view themselves. For example, the study asked how they viewed themselves politically—did they identify as liberal or conservative or something in between? Did they consider themselves religious? And did giving to charity change based on any of those factors? Or did any of these factors change what types of charities received money? Did self-identified liberals give differently than conservatives, for example? Did nonreligious people give differently, either in amount or type of charity, than religious people? Was it a correct assumption that high income people gave more than low income people and did they give to similar causes?

The study gave real insight into charitable giving patterns in the United States. The results are very useful in talking about giving to private charities, those identified by the government to be tax exempt because of their charitable purpose.

As mentioned, after matching charitable giving with individuals, the study examined giving among several demographic groups and one of those were people who identified themselves as religious. For that study, "religious" was defined as people who said that they attended religious services at least twenty-seven times a year, or on average at least every other week a year. The converse, for the purposes of the study, those that attended religious services less than twenty-seven times a year and were termed "nonreligious".

When comparing giving patterns, the study found several interesting trends. For our purposes, we'll look at giving related to religious individuals and religious organizations.

The data showed that those who identified themselves as religious gave more to charity than those who did not see themselves as religious. That may not be surprising, but the difference certainly was, at least to this author. The results found that not only did self-identified religious people give more to charity than self-identified nonreligious people, they gave significantly more. The study found that religious people gave roughly four times more to charitable causes than those who were nonreligious.

That finding and difference in charitable giving is large

enough that one could not be blamed for finding it hard to believe. Yet, even if the data were off ... by a lot, there would still be quite a difference and the overall trend would not change.

However, even if we would acknowledge that religious people give several times more to charities than those who are not religious, there is an obvious question: how much of that charitable giving is to religious causes and done to further certain religious beliefs and so maybe do not benefit others?

The purpose of this writing is not necessarily to discuss the pros and cons of religion, in and of itself. However, having said that and whether for right or wrong, someone who is not religious or may be agnostic or atheistic, they would see little value in giving to religious charities. As a result, they would discount that aspect of charitable giving to some degree, depending on the person's personal views and the passion with which they held them.

Fortunately, the study was comprehensive enough that there is data that answers that question: how much of the charitable giving of religious people went to primarily religious charities? What it tells us is enlightening. The data included what types of charities were the beneficiaries of the giving, and that information was linked to the people in the study so that it could be examined in multiple ways. When the study took out donations to religious charities and looked solely at nonreligious charitable giving, the findings were the same though obviously not quite as overwhelmingly so.

When only measuring giving that went to nonreligious or secular causes, people who identified themselves as religious still gave more to charity than others. So even if you would take out the money given to churches, synagogues, and other religious groups, a larger percentage of people who were religious gave to other, secular charities than those who were not religious. Said another way, the type of charity did not change the overall financial trend of giving patterns between religious and nonreligious individuals, although it obviously changed the magnitude of the difference.

To get a better understanding of the breadth of the data, let's look at it in a couple of different ways that expand or provide more detail. Reviewing giving *only to nonreligious charitable causes*, we can review how many people gave and also how much they donated when they did give.

When looking at the population of people who said they were religious and the population of people who said they were not religious, a higher proportion of people who were religious donated money to charities. A total of 15 percent more of those who were religious gave to charity than those who were not religious. Said another way, out of every one hundred people in each of these groups, fifteen more in the religious group gave money to nonreligious charities than did people in the nonreligious group.

In addition to more people giving, the amount of money given to nonreligious charities was also higher. When they did give, the study found that religious individuals gave an average of 20 percent more than nonreligious people to secular charities. So 15 percent more religious people gave to secular charities and when they did so, they gave 20 percent more money. And that is after taking out money given to religious charities and is also without accounting for the income level of those involved.

That is a significant difference. Even when you back out

donations to charities that are primarily religious in nature, a higher percentage of individuals who consider themselves religious give to charity and, of those that do, they give a higher amount of money to charity than those who are not religious. So it is clear that, at least in the area of giving to private charities, there is a clear difference in giving patterns. Religious beliefs directly relate to people's actions when it comes to charitable giving.

That is not to be critical of people who are not religious. Giving to charity and giving back is a personal decision. However, the data does say that there is something about people's religious views that influences their charitable giving. The data is so clear that it must indicate something fundamental to the differences in belief systems that relates to charitable giving. Additionally, the difference is large enough and spread across the whole country, so that it cannot be considered an outlier.

What would account for that? The study did not delve into that question so we can only speculate at some level. Whether it be Jesus' admonition to help the poor and destitute, the Apostle Paul's direction for the church to help widows, the ancient Jewish custom to leave some of your crops in the field so the poor could feed themselves or some other reason, the end result is the same. More people who practice their religious views by attending a place of worship regularly give to charity, and when they do they give more. Significantly more. And that is after they have already given to their religious cause.

In a very tangible sense, religious people provide a benefit to the society at large. In this case, a financial benefit that is significant and quantifiable.

If we would use charitable giving as a measure of giving back or helping others who are less fortunate, there is an advantage that society receives from people who are religious that can be measured and quantified. As it relates to giving to charitable causes, there is a secular case for religion.

Three

Medical Care

When we think of how to help others, there may be no need more basic than help for the sick and infirmed. Correspondingly, perhaps in no other area is the benefit of religious organizations to society more readily evident than in caring for the sick and ill.

At a high level we can look at casual yet obvious evidence of this. In New York City, the largest city in the United States, the largest hospitals have such names as Presbyterian and Mount Sinai Beth Israel, a testament to the influence and dedication of resources by Christian and Jewish religious groups in establishing hospitals to care for the sick.

New York Presbyterian is the largest hospital in the country but is there a city of any size in the country that doesn't have a hospital with a reference to its founding by religious charities: St Luke's, Methodist, Baptist, St. Vincent's, St. Jude, Good Samaritan or others? For the author, growing up in a small suburban Midwestern town of about ten thousand people, the local hospital was St.

Alphonsus, a Catholic hospital that was, at that time, the only one to serve the whole county.

The sheer number and breadth of such places gives evidence to the enormity of resources dedicated by religious organizations to the care for the sick. Especially in the early years of our country, in many cities and towns the only hospitals were those that had their roots in religious organizations. The same could be said for other parts of the world.

Over the years, the governmental and regulatory environment has changed in the US and even more so in Europe. The partnerships, mergers and changes in the medical landscape have made analysis somewhat less clear cut, but even with these changes estimates are that over 40 percent of the hospitals in the United States are still affiliated with religious organizations, at least at some level.

For example, of the ten largest hospital systems (measured by total number of beds), five of those have affiliation with religious organizations or began as religious ministries (Presbyterian in New York being the largest).

In several Western countries today, health care is nationalized and provided by the government. Yet in many places that have government run health care, such as Great Britain and Canada, there are still private hospitals that operate and a large portion of the independent hospitals that are not run by the government are run by religious organizations.

In a number of Third World countries where healthcare is not as readily available, religious and missionary organizations offer the only medical facilities in whole regions of the country or even the continent. One example was mentioned above, a hospital in Togo, Africa founded by a Baptist Christian organization. The Hospital of Hope serves patients from this poor region of Africa including people from Togo, Benin, Burkina Faso, Ghana, Niger, and Nigeria.

One of the few hospitals in Togo, the opening of the hospital brought the President of the country to the ribbon cutting. The hospital offers comprehensive services. It has an outpatient clinic that includes a dental room for use when dentists are available. It is equipped with x-ray and ultrasound equipment, a lab and full pharmacy, a neonatal intensive care unit, isolation rooms and an infectious ward, four operating rooms and sixty-five inpatient beds. In a country where the indigenous medical infrastructure is sparse, the Hospital of Hope tries to fill a critical gap for those who are underserved.

As importantly, the Hospital of Hope has also set up a training facility and curriculum to train nurses, so that they can provide ongoing and growing medical support for this underserved region. Through this effort, they hope to build a human infrastructure that will make the people of the region more self-sustaining and not totally dependent on others for meeting their medical needs.

The same Christian organization that founded and built that hospital in Togo, also did the same thing in a poor and underserved area of Bangladesh. In that case, the hospital was founded and began ministering to people when that country was still part of Pakistan and continued to minister to the sick and injured during the civil war that eventually resulted in the independence of Bangladesh. Over decades that hospital, started by a Christian missionary organization, has served an area and people who, to this day, often lack the basics of medical care.

At each of the hospitals mentioned above, the medical professionals-doctors and nurses-are primarily long and short term volunteers serving with a Christian missionary organization. These clinicians are people of faith and religious conviction, who give their lives to serve at these and other similar hospitals and medical facilities around the world. They forego what would be much more lucrative and financially rewarding careers to serve in these underprivileged and poorly served areas. For these individuals, their belief in serving others and living their lives in accordance with their religious conviction is a higher priority than the money that they could receive if they chose a different path.

The examples above would seemingly make it self-evident that, at least in this area, money given to religious charities and organizations flows through to benefit society, as a whole, whether religious or not. When taking even a casual notice of hospitals and clinics that care for the sick, we can see the impact of religious groups around the world, and certainly in the United States. In this area, there can be little doubt that there is a secular case to be made for religion and the impact religion has on the communities around them.

These examples have a long historical tradition, as well. For those who may be interested in a bit of history, this is one area where there is a long story to tell, if only briefly for our purposes.

Since ancient times, we read in history books of provisions made to care for the sick among almost every major religion. Using Christianity as an example, care for the sick, diseased and injured and the establishment of what would become hospitals has a long history, going back almost to the beginning of the religion itself.

At the highest level, the foundation and example for this type of care for others was laid when Jesus himself spent a good portion of his ministry helping the sick. We can easily draw the parallel that this evidences itself in the extent to which Christians and Christian organizations have placed on serving their communities with hospitals and medical facilities to care for the sick.

Christianity was outlawed in the Roman Empire for much of its early history. The Roman Emperor Constantine was the first to legalize the practice of Christianity. Within a generation, caring for the sick became a fundamental tenet of the (then) upstart religion. St. Basil of Cappadocia established a religious order dedicated to helping the poor and sick. The order set up what we would think of as a hospital, with an area to house lepers, and separate buildings to house the other sick and the poor.

Early in the 5th century, St. Benedict of Nursia founded a religious order that put the care for the sick as the priority among its Christian duties. It is from this beginning that one of the very first medical schools grew up in Salerno, Italy. Indeed, the Benedictine monastic order carried on this tradition for hundreds of years

Religion continued to be the dominant influence in the establishment of hospitals in Europe through the latter years of the Roman Empire and through the Middle Ages. Hospitals in every country in Europe were primarily run by churches, and medical care and training, such as it was, was done through religious groups.

Religious institutions continued to run most of the hospitals in Europe until Henry VIII of England seized the assets of the Catholic Church between 1536-1540, including the hospitals. However, even after hospitals began to change their organization in England, religious groups such as the Huguenots still ministered to the sick and Huguenots established a hospital there in 1718, for example.

Early hospitals in what was to become the United States were often places to help the sick, as well as to help the poor. One of the first was established by the early Quaker and colonial leader William Penn, who established a hospital in 1713. From those beginnings, churches and synagogues continued to establish hospitals and clinics to care for the sick in a rapidly growing country. In cities and towns across the nation, we see that legacy still today.

Four

Children's Homes And Shelters

Perhaps there is no more tragic ongoing situation in the world than that of a child who does not have a home or a place to live where they can grow up and just be loved. Unfortunately, too many children not only lack a place to be loved but actually live in places where they live in fear. Maybe it is fear of a parent who struggles with addiction and puts their addiction above everything, including the well-being of their children. Or maybe it's a tragedy of having lost a parent to violence. Or maybe worse, having parents who just did not care, did not want the responsibility and just walked away.

Whatever the case, there are children in the world who fall through the cracks and have no place to go to get a good meal and have a safe place to lay their head at night. In Florida alone, for example, there are over 22,000 children in the foster care system at any given time.

Churches and religious groups often fill the gap.

I, personally, have been fortunate in many ways, and among them is that I have not had to face such challenges and have not had close friends that had to go through those types of hardship. Yet, before I was born, my parents worked at an orphanage (as it was called at the time) and home for children. Later in life, I had friends who spent years as house parents at a children's home and so I heard first hand stories, and sometimes saw up close, the challenges that these children face and the unique needs that they have.

When I had friends who worked with the kids in the children's home, I had a chance to meet and spend some time with some of the children. Many times, these friends would bring some of the children that they lived with to church with them or to other social functions. Several of us would periodically help out by spending an afternoon doing things with the girls from the home, such as playing volleyball or kickball or some other activity. From time to time we might take them small gifts, which always amazed me because the smallest things seemed so special to them.

A short aside just to share how seemingly simple things are important things to children in need. As I said, a group of us from our church would sometimes do things for the girls that our friends lived with as house parents. On one occasion, we went to play some kickball and games on a weekend afternoon and also took along some food. Not that they were necessarily going hungry but as a donation to the home and maybe some snacks that they wouldn't ordinarily get. Among the food and snacks were several boxes of cereal, just different varieties of breakfast cereal that seemed to be nothing out of the ordinary. Yet all these years later I have never forgotten the reaction of one young lady. One of the youngsters, a 17-year old girl, was helping unload the boxes of food and snacks, set it down on the counter and looked at the cereal. She thanked us profusely. The person standing next to her gave a simple "You're welcome." To which the young lady responded, "No, really, thank you. You don't understand. This stuff is like gold around here."

Though each home had a refrigerator and small table, there was a dining hall that each of the several group homes on the campus went to at each meal time. I don't know if the box of cereal was a treat because that meant that they could eat breakfast in their home instead of walking over to the dining hall or what was the reason that a simple box of cereal was such a big deal. I was too stunned at the time to ask but it made such a lasting impression on me that for years, even after my friends were no longer house parents there, I would go at night on Christmas Eve with a trunk full of snacks, which always included several boxes of cereal, and just leave them on the front porch of that home. If such a simple thing, something that I just take for granted, could be a special treat for some child, then that was a very simple thing for me to do and a very simple way to say 'thank you' for what I had.

That story illustrated for me the size of the need for those children and it obviously stuck with me years later. Even the simplest things were unusual for those youngsters. Things most of us take for granted were special treats.

That home for children there in Florida was a vivid example to me of how churches and religious groups help children who are likely at the lowest points of their lives, having to deal with things that no child should have to deal with. That particular home, and a handful like it around the state, were founded and run by a group of Baptist churches. That religious organization, years before, had seen a need to help others-in this case the most vulnerable among us-and set up homes where children who had no other options could go to live. And, if nothing changed, they could live there until they were eighteen and then they would be given help to get a job and a place of their own. All along the way, these children had the benefit of a stable environment, a safe place to go each night, encouragement and counseling, as many came from challenging and disturbing circumstances. It certainly isn't a perfect way to grow up, but it's much better than they had and it gives them a chance to grow up, get schooling and prepare to make a life that they might not have had a chance to ever see if they had been forced to stay in their circumstances.

One of the really good things about organizations such as these, is that when they grow they use the growth and additional funds to expand their services to reach more people. This particular children's home in Florida has significantly expanded its reach with additional services. There are now several campuses and homes throughout the state of Florida, and they have expanded the types of services that they offer. They now work with state agencies to help children who are victims of sex trafficking and have established a home especially for these victims to hide out and get help with their specific needs. Additionally, they have used their organizational experience to begin ministering in Haiti, the poorest country in the hemisphere. They have established a home for children in that country. Additionally, on top of establishing a home to serve children in Haiti, they organize and coordinate regular teams of people that travel at their own expense to go help the staff there serve the needs of children there in Haiti.

The impact on those children physically, emotionally, and socially, of finding an option like that during their formative years may never be fully known. And the investment in those young lives not only helps the children directly, but helps us all by taking at-risk kids and giving them an alternative to lifestyle choices that likely would, at a minimum, perpetuate the bad situations that they came from. Although we could certainly guess at some of the impact and read testimonials from those involved who are now grown, we can probably never fully know the value that comes from the investments in those children.

However, in more tangible terms, we can give some measure to the contribution which that group of churches makes to the well-being of the children they serve.

Using that one example above of the Baptist Children's Home there in Florida, solely because it's one I'm most familiar with, we can put a dollar amount to that work. In the most recent year (as of this writing), that organization spent roughly $26 million[1] ministering to children. It's a bit hard to get comprehensive data or to extrapolate accurately, but that figure is for the state of Florida, for one year, by that one particular religious organization and that one denomination. That's a significant amount that goes to help those children who otherwise would have little or no hope.

The majority of that money comes from churches. Part of the charitable contributions from individuals to churches go meet this need in the community and, as such, it is an example of a nonreligious benefit of churches and religious groups to the communities around them. A secular case for religion.

---

[1] "Annual Report, 2019", Florida Baptist Children's Home.

Five

Homeless Shelters

Of course, homelessness does not just affect children. Most recently, the rise of the pandemic crisis and the associated economic devastation has seen the problem of homelessness rise dramatically.

In Jacksonville, Florida, there is a church that established a homeless shelter. As that church saw a need years ago, they established a place in the downtown area to serve as a shelter for those in need. The staff at this shelter is considered part of the staff of the church itself and is paid primarily through church funds, as are most of the other expenses. The shelter provides temporary housing to hundreds and serves up tens of thousands of meals each year for those in need.

As that church worked to help address the immediate needs of homelessness, the church realized that there was a gap in the needs of the homeless that they served, which were primarily men. So they invested significant additional resources and also established a women and children's shelter. This facility was dedicated solely to meeting the unique needs of that part of the homeless population that includes women with young children. As you can imagine, the additional needs for children ranging from infants to teenagers make the challenges even more significant. Layer in the need for kids to keep up with education to keep them from falling even farther behind and having the problems become self-perpetuating, and we just begin to understand the additional resources needed to adequately address the needs of this population.

However, this church was determined to help provide long-term solutions and not just help with the symptoms of the problem. So the church does not just stop at meeting the immediate needs of food and shelter and has set up a program and provided significant facilities for rehabilitation and vocational training with the goal of helping the homeless become self-supporting so that they have a hope for life going forward. The church has developed a program that lasts several months, with milestones and requirements along the way, which helps people develop work skills and change habits that get in the way of being self-sufficient. One of the mechanisms the church has set up is a tract of land where they have a 'Freedom Farm'. The farm has a place where people in the program can live, and also provides a place where residents can work, learn job skills, and earn a living that will eventually get them to the point where they are able to re-enter the workforce completely, to live lives that maintain their dignity and which allow them to support themselves and their families.

In an absolutely heartwarming event each year, there is a special evening service right before Thanksgiving where the church turns the service over to the people in the program and the staff. For a while that evening, people who have been helped and whose hope is dramatically different than just a year earlier get a chance to share how their lives have changed and what they are thankful for during the holiday season. The life stories and thankfulness of those individuals for a new opportunity is something that touches deep into your heart. If you are ever in the area of Jacksonville, FL during that week, and want something to lift your spirits and to show you what it's like to have hope restored, and maybe just bring a tear to your eye, you should stop in to hear these amazing people.

This church is not unique. In fact, in most cities the homeless shelters have been founded and are run by churches and religious organizations. Although somewhat of a stereotype, the image of the doors of city rescue missions underneath signs that read 'Jesus Saves' belies the fact that religious charities have a long history for aiding the homeless and destitute.

Yet that stereotypical image also is indicative of something that makes religious groups uniquely positioned to help in the battle against homelessness. Data will show that many, though certainly not all, of those that are fighting homelessness are also struggling with other issues in their lives, which may include substance abuse and addiction. Religious groups use approaches that involve a moral component that often incorporate ways to seek help and guidance from God. Though some who are not religious, or maybe anti-religious, would debate that evidence, there is a lot that supports the view that this unique moral aspect helps. The solace that one's religion or spiritual practice provides in times of difficulty can be particularly important to an individual battling an addiction or substance abuse problem.

The traditional 12-step program originally developed in the 1930's was developed with an acknowledgement of and desire for help from God. The program has moved away from a direct reference to 'God' and now uses the term 'higher power' but this basic outline has been incorporated into a number of religiously-based treatment programs that have been developed and used with success over time. One of these, "Celebrate Recovery", has become widely used within Christian church groups in recent years and has seen promising results in supporting people in their struggles with addiction.

In addition to a good deal of anecdotal evidence, there is also clinical evidence of improved outcomes. Though results are often hard to measure, in part because of the anonymous nature of the programs, one study from 2019 which reviewed several years of data from various programs, supports the view that faith-based programs provide better outcomes when dealing with addiction and working through recovery.[2]

While not as directly tangible in talking about how religious charities and groups help in combatting homelessness, it is significant and noteworthy that religion of itself helps this population, as well. If improved outcomes in combatting addictions are seen through the introduction of a spiritual or moral component brought by faith-based programs, society will benefit as much or more as from the strictly financial investment in combatting homelessness.

In the battle against homelessness and its causes, there is a benefit to society from the efforts of churches and religious groups: a clear secular case for religion.

---

[2] Hai, Audrey Hang, Franklin, Cynthia et al, "The efficacy of spiritual/religious interventions for substance use problems: A systematic review and meta-analysis of randomized controlled trials", *Drug and Alcohol Dependence,* 202 (2019), 134-148.

Six

Sex Trafficking

Sex trafficking is a problem that often lurks in the shadows, combining the worst parts of humanity: enslavement of other people along with exploitation of another person and their body solely for financial gain of the trafficker. Only in the last couple of years, with news headlines of the crimes of Jeffrey Epstein, have many people come to realize how such heinous actions are sometimes hidden in plain sight.

The growth of the commercial sex industry in recent years has also helped fuel the problem. As the shame in society of involvement in the sex industry has lessened, the problem of trafficking has grown inversely. Despite protestations that these are harmless occupations and innocent crimes, the commercial sex industry and sex trafficking are interrelated businesses that prey on the vulnerable. Though hard to measure for obvious reasons, estimates range anywhere from a third to two-thirds of 'sex workers'-people who work in the commercial sex industry-are victims of trafficking. Looking at it from the opposite view, estimates say that roughly 70 percent of female trafficking victims are trafficked into the commercial sex industry, meaning that they are working in porn, escorting, massage parlors, strip clubs and the like.

It's a problem that is rampant, even here in the United States. Government best estimates suggest that over 300,000 US citizens are forced into prostitution/trafficking each year and, even more appalling, the average overall age of those trafficked is seventeen. If we only look at victims who are not yet adults, the average age that a teen enters the sex trade in the US is twelve to fourteen years old, with many of these being runaway girls who were sexually abused as children.[3]

Shaped, in part, by movies such as *Taken* the stereotypical view of sex trafficking is of someone who is taken, transported far away from their home and then forced to work as sex objects. Yet that is not the most common situation. The majority of victims are drawn into sex trafficking close to their homes, at the most vulnerable points in their lives.

And trafficking occurs not just in big cities and large metropolitan areas but even in rural towns. Domestic human trafficking is documented in all seventy-two counties of Wisconsin, for example. It is just as prevalent in the north woods where it is sometimes easier for traffickers to blend in and hide as it is in the metro Milwaukee area.

Such was the story of Tiffany, whose story is shared in more detail because of the vivid, shocking nature found in this area of tragedy and need, which is often hidden from most of us. And because of the horrific nature of the

---

[3] "Human Trafficking Within and Into the United States: A Review of the Literature." Office of the Assistant Secretary for Planning and Evaluation. Accessed July 31, 2019, https://aspe.hhs.gov/report/human-trafficking-and-within-united-states-review-literature#Trafficking.

story, it also illustrates the especially unique and critical help required.

Tiffany testified in a federal sex trafficking case in Dodge County, Wisconsin.[4] She was a certified nursing assistant when her father passed away when she was twenty-four. A neighbor who the family knew in passing, Christopher Childs, befriended her during this vulnerable period. Childs offered to get her a job at 'The Hardware Store', which was a local gentlemen's club, to help make more money during this difficult time in her life. After all, it was just a strip club and he promised to help make sure her family was taken care of. Tiffany said that she did not realize that Childs was already laying the groundwork for her to be totally dependent on him.

Later, Tiffany testified, he forced her to quit her job as a CNA and work for him full time. "At the beginning, you aren't getting beaten, at the beginning you aren't getting physically forced to do anything. It's the mental manipulation," said Tiffany.

Tiffany said Childs eventually controlled everything in her life. He decided what she ate, when she slept and when she worked. Childs would keep tabs on her and other women at the clubs he sent them to, even if he wasn't there and the penalty for not doing what she was told was steep.

"I was sodomized with a hot curling iron," said Tiffany. "He strangled women to the point of passing out."

---

[4] Background from Klopf, Rebecca, "I Made Damn Sure I Was the Last", *Milwaukee Journal-Sentinel*, November 12, 2020, accessed December 12, 2020, https://www.tmj4.com/news/local-news/i-made-damn-sure-i-was-the-last-survivor-shares-story-after-turning-in-man-who-abused-her-for-years

During the trial, other victims testified they were beaten, forced to sleep outside in the snow, and even branded with Childs' name. There was also graphic testimony about the horrific sexual torture including times when Childs' would have a friend rape and beat someone who disobeyed him.

Childs eventually pled guilty to sex trafficking, admitting that he raped, tortured and sold nearly a dozen women, including Tiffany. The owner of the strip club and two former employees were also convicted along with Childs.

The courage it took to leave despite the threats, and then to testify against the trafficking ring must have been unimaginable.

Through Tiffany's trial, she had support from Krista Hull, President and Founder of Redeem and Restore Center (RRC), a local Christian organization that battles sex trafficking. To take on a group of traffickers when you are vulnerable and have nothing to your name, as Tiffany did, is a momentous decision. Moral support to make such a decision and step out at great personal risk is important. Krista and RRC were there to lend support during the trial, to lend encouragement during the long period of time leading up to the trail and to walk beside her when the weight of her decision seemed overwhelming.

People who spend years of their lives, with every aspect controlled by someone else, with every dollar of their money taken from them and with threats of violence and death hanging over them every minute, have so many other things that they must deal with even if they are able to break free from their enslavement. Even when they break free or, as in the case above, even after the trafficker's trial is over, the victim's struggle is just beginning. They have to rebuild their lives in pretty much every conceivable way after spending years where everything about their lives and their environment was controlled by someone else.

Because of the many types and layers of trauma these victims have endured, there is a need to stand by them and help them to make new lives after they have left and are no longer enslaved. In many cases, these victims were trafficked while still teenagers and so have known nothing about supporting themselves or living on their own as adults. Life and job skills need to be learned, to say nothing of the ongoing psychological trauma that they must feel and endure.

That is the mission of Redeem and Restore Center, the Christian-based organization that Krista heads in Wisconsin: to support and walk alongside women that have experienced trafficking or exploitation, providing or connecting them with resources that help with their individual needs for physical, emotional, psychological and relational support. Victims need a complex and comprehensive set of services to help prepare them for a life that is new to them, without which they will be in a vulnerable position that likely led them to fall victim in the first place. Such a thing as feeling safe, away from the threat of violence or someone coming to get you after you escaped seems so simple to most of us, but is just the beginning of a long process of restoration for individuals who are victims of things most of us cannot even imagine.

Additionally and unfortunately, we are becoming increasingly aware of the problem of sex trafficking as it relates to children and the predators who traffic in pedophilia.

Though those who deal with children had been aware of the growing problem, many of us only realized the potential extent of the issue with the case of Jeffrey Epstein and his rich friends who used their money to prey on young girls. As mentioned earlier, the average age of someone trapped in sex trafficking is seventeen and among young people that fall victim, they are often runaway girls as young as twelve to fourteen. That is frighteningly young.

The horrific case of Epstein and his enablers and friends has certainly been an eye-opener to something that probably few of us knew was as pervasive as it appears now to be.

Children's services are moving into this much needed area, serving kids who are victims of human sex trafficking. For example, we spoke earlier of a children's home in Florida. Within the last few years, the home has expanded its services, as have many others, to include combating child trafficking and helping the young victims of that disgusting industry. As could be imagined, these children have needs that are even more intensive and specialized than other children in their care. The infrastructure needed is more expansive and in depth, and in a time of tight government budgets there is a gap that religious organizations are moving to help fill. In Florida, that includes building a safe house for rescued child sex traffic victims that is secret and not publicized. The Baptist Children's Home works with the State of Florida to provide a home to begin the process of recovery, after law enforcement has intervened to get a child to safety.

As is the case with other victims of sex trafficking, the needs for these victims are broad and wide-ranging. As we can imagine, this is even more so when the victim is a child. The trauma they experience, in their young and formative years, magnifies the impact on them and makes it infinitely more difficult to adjust to a life of feeling safe and able to trust.

The two examples above are just part of a broader picture of what religious and faith-based groups are doing. There are many others. These groups work to not just combat sex trafficking but to stand with victims, to help them recover and position themselves to live their lives in a way that gives them hope for tomorrow. A hope that many of them may not ever have had.

When charitable donations go to churches, synagogues and religious organizations, part of that goes to help people like Tiffany and to help children caught in the slavery of sex trafficking. To these people, there is a secular benefit for religion.

Seven

Human Trafficking And Slavery

Taking it up one more level, to the context of human trafficking which may or may not be related to the sex trade, again we find religious organizations that step in to battle modern slavery (after all, 'trafficking' is just another way to say 'slavery', where one person owns and controls another as property). As much as we think that slavery is a relic of the past, it still is a part of life in several parts of the world and, unfortunately it is a part of life for some even in the United States.

In places such as sub-Saharan Africa and certain parts of Asia, there are long-standing problems with human trafficking. Often this is related to wars or tribal disputes where either defeated people are enslaved by victorious armies or are driven away from their homes with nothing to live on and so are forced to do whatever is necessary in order to survive. Yet, these are not the only reasons for the human trafficking problem around the world.

Poverty is often a driver of human trafficking. High poverty rates due to lack of economic development and growth, limited job opportunities and inadequate education lead many people to look for opportunities in other countries through illegal immigration and third party brokers. Even in the United States, poverty-stricken areas with generational challenges along the same lines leave people vulnerable. Traffickers prey upon these vulnerable people and provide an initial glimmer of hope for a way out. Yet far too often, hopes are crushed when these desperate people find themselves unexpectedly forced into de-facto slavery.

Human trafficking is the fastest growing criminal industry in the world, generating more than $150 billion each year according to estimates from several organizations that attempt to track the problem. According to the UN's International Labor Organization, an estimated forty million people are victims of modern slavery. Of those, they say that one in four are children[5]. The majority of the enslaved people are used for forced labor in industries such as agriculture, garment production and the sex industry.

Those figures boggle the mind. If the figure of forty million people being enslaved in the world today is roughly accurate, that's more than the population of most countries and roughly equal to the population of the entire state of California, the largest state in the US. How could that many people be enslaved in this, the 21st century? The simple magnitude of the problem makes it one which would seem almost insurmountable.

Yet, there are a number of religious groups working to heal those rescued from slavery and human trafficking across the globe. Among these groups, at least one is trying a slightly different approach.

---

[5] "Our Work", Freedompromise.org.

Started with assistance from a church in middle Tennessee, Freedom's Promise works in Cambodia on long term solutions to human trafficking. To solve the problems long term, the emphasis is on reducing vulnerability and on establishing ways to build prevention by focusing on root causes of the problem. When security and basic necessities are missing, that gives an opportunity for traffickers to fill the gaps by preying on individuals desperately seeking a way to survive. This organization works with local leaders to provide infrastructure assistance such as health care, education and vocational help for at-risk populations. There is a team of individuals in the United States that works with a team of individuals in Cambodia to identify needs and opportunities within communities there. Working together, these teams coordinate financial and volunteer resources to apply on those areas of need and to the people affected.

The focus on prevention and addressing the root causes that lead to vulnerability, which then leads to victimization by traffickers is showing results. According to Freedom's Promise, in communities where they work they have seen tremendous success, reducing human trafficking by up to roughly 60%. That is an impressive result, meaning more than half of the people that historically may have fallen into trafficking now have other opportunities that provide them hope and an alternative to a live of enslavement. Of course, these results are in certain small areas where they work and the problem is widespread and worldwide. However to those people impacted, that isn't a small thing and is indeed life changing.

With roots in a Tennessee church and the financial giving to that church from individuals, Freedom's Promise is having an impact across the globe. There has been a measureable benefit to the world from those beginnings. The work of Freedom's Promise is evidence that there is a benefit to society that has resulted from money given to that church and it makes a secular case for religion.

Eight

Serving Special Needs

Several years ago, there was a church in Milwaukee that had organized, traditional Sunday School groups. In one of those groups, the people became friends and spent time together outside of church. As you might expect, over time they became good friends, their families became friends and they formed a bond. Among those friends from that church were parents of a special needs child.

Unless you are around a child with special needs or have one within your family, it is hard to imagine the level of care required. After a while, it became clear to this group of friends the great amount of time and effort it took to care for that special child, far more than their own neurotypical children, for sure. Children will keep parents busy under most circumstances but add in unique physical, emotional and educational needs and it can become almost overwhelming.

As they saw first-hand what their friends dealt with daily, this group decided they wanted to do something. If nothing else, they could just give them a break to take some time for themselves now and then. The group began to help these parents with just the occasional night out, while the group took turns and cared for their special child.

After a while, this became a habit that grew. As these friends gained awareness, they began to notice more when they came in contact with other families and individuals with special needs. Among the group was a doctor, who more fully understood the additional physical challenges that were often involved. The group realized that there was a bigger need around them that wasn't being met, that there were others with special needs whose families were struggling pretty much by themselves, and they decided to try to do something about it.

The group took their heart-felt burden to the broader church and to key people in the congregation. Before long, plans were being made to expand the effort to help. . At that time, little was being done in public education to address needs of those with intellectual disabilities. So the goal evolved and grew into one that would encompass helping with both the physical and the educational needs that were unique to this population. Within just a few years Shepherd's Home and School became a reality; a residential home for those with special needs. As Shepherd's accepted its first residents, the need became more obvious and families from across the country reached out to Shepherd's for help. The need was large and work grew. As it did, Shepherd's ministry expanded to include additional education and emotional support. It began to include vocational training and partnering with local businesses to find jobs where these special people could achieve their appropriate level of independence. Local businesses found, with some patience, the help of Shepherd's staff and training which incorporated employer feedback that these individuals could become loyal and dependable employees when matched with the correct job. The partnerships between the school, the individuals and local business would become a classic 'win-win' for all involved. Residents would find employment and a life that took advantage of their potential, while local businesses had a dependable workforce to draw from which had an infrastructure for support, and the community benefited from the partnership.

Decades later, that church still ministers in the Milwaukee area and Shepherd's campus in Union Grove, WI is still helping those who have special needs and unique challenges. The Shepherd's facility has transformed into a college that provides more advanced vocational training for people of special needs. Shepherd's College has become the leading three year post-secondary educational program serving people with special needs in the country. They offer programs in culinary arts, health care and basic office skills and then help students with finding employment. The whole program is designed with the goal helping these students find a level of independence that is appropriate to their abilities, and which promotes their self-worth and dignity.

Everything in that example began with a traditional Sunday School class at one church. From that one small church group, over the years hundreds of individuals with special needs have led more complete lives than they could have, and their families have been better equipped to deal with the challenges involved in helping their loved ones reach their full potential.

There is an ongoing benefit to the community and to society from the charity of that church and its people. A secular case for religion.

Nine

Education And Learning

Besides caring for the sick, perhaps no other part of society has been impacted by religion and the investment of resources to the extent, and for as long of a period of time, as that of education and learning. Some, if not most, of the Western world's greatest universities have their origins in religion. We see that across the globe, and it doesn't take long to think of examples.

The Sorbonne in France was founded by the French theologian Robert de Sorbon, who was also confessor to King Louis IX.

Oxford is the oldest university in the English-speaking world and the second oldest continuously operating in the world. Many colleges at Oxford University had religious beginnings. Exeter College was founded for students from the Exeter Diocese. Lincoln College was founded by the Archbishop of Lincoln to train students in theology. All Souls College was founded by Archbishop Chichelle and on and on.

Here is the United States, both Harvard and Yale, founded before the United States had even become a country, had their roots in religion and were founded to train students in religion and theology.

Harvard is the oldest institution of higher learning in the United States. Founded in 1636, it was originally envisioned as a place to train clergy for the growing Puritan population of the Massachusetts Bay Colony and was named after John Harvard, the young minister who was its first benefactor.

Yale traces its roots to the 1640's when local clergy led an effort to found an institution of higher learning. Receiving official charter by the Connecticut Colony in 1701, it was intended to prepare students for lives as Congregational ministers and its curriculum originally offered in theology and sacred languages.

Most widely known for its religious affiliation in the US these days is probably Notre Dame, founded in 1842. It is a traditionally Catholic school, whose President is always a Catholic priest, and is also a major research university. Similarly, Baylor University is a Baptist university founded in 1845 by a group of churches in Texas. It was one of the first schools of higher education west of the Mississippi River and is the oldest continuously operating university in Texas.

The list could go on, with the point being that churches and religious groups, and the money donated to them, have been instrumental in advancing education in the United States and around the world.. Each of the institutions mentioned certainly had their part in religious education and training ministers and lay people to serve, but in each case they have expanded their scope and provide education among a very broad range of fields, and from their halls have come some of the finest minds across every area of society.

The colleges and universities in the United States and

Western Europe that were formed by churches and religious groups are numerous and several readily come to mind. Among elementary education, we also find a number of schools formed and run by churches. In every part of the country, churches run schools to educate young people with many having reputations for high levels of achievement.

As widespread as these examples are, efforts to promote education by churches and religious groups are not just locally or nationally focused. There are a group of churches, for example, that work with an organization called Every Girl Counts. This group is dedicated to helping impoverished girls in Kenya reach their full potential, by bringing education resources to girls who would not have any other opportunity to learn.

In 2016, Every Girl Counts began offering educational opportunities to some of the brightest and most needy girls. Starting with 30 girls in Nairobi, Kenya, the number has grown each year since then in the belief that education means empowerment, which can be a sustainable way to lift people out of poverty and despair. In this small but growing way, Every Girl Counts is using education to address long-term generational problems.

As that work to bring education to young women in Kenya has begun to grow, there are similar examples in other places that are making an impact in local communities around the world.

Whether it be in the world of higher education, elementary education or in basic literacy, the history of the investment in education by faith-based groups is long and ongoing. In this country and others, there has been a benefit to society from that investment, a secular case for religion.

Ten

And Yet More

We have talked about a number of different areas where religious-affiliated charities are making an impact on the people and communities around them, quite apart from any direct religious work or effort. And, frankly, the list could go on to cover more areas that are as broad as the areas of need.

We could talk about a group called 'Living Water for Roatan', for example. The group works in Roatan, Honduras, the second poorest country in Central America, to provide permanent sources of clean drinking water while also sharing their religious message of 'living water'.

There are also groups that stand ready to help when natural disasters strike. When a hurricane, tornado or in this time of pandemic, you will find these groups going to help the areas most impacted. One of these, Samaritan's Purse, brought truckloads of supplies and staff to Nashville when several tornados hit the area in early 2020. They set up a mobile hospital in Central Park in New York City and rallied clinical staff during that city's darkest hours of the pandemic.

There are long serving groups that have a religious foundation that have been in most of our communities for so long, we often don't think of their religious origins or basis. Groups such as the YMCA and YWCA (Young Men's/Women's Christian Association), the Salvation Army and others. These groups show the long historical record of churches and people of faith working to serve the communities around them and to help those in need.

Though we have been talking primarily about giving direct physical and material aid to those in need, we have also seen the impact of religion, churches and synagogues in fighting injustice and social ills. The instance that most readily comes to mind is the leadership of clergy during the most challenging days of the civil rights struggles in the United States and also in other places. Rev. Martin Luther King Jr. was the most prominent leader in the fight for civil rights and non-violence. King was pastor of Ebenezer Baptist Church and led the movement for civil rights and literally gave his life for it. Other key figures were also driven, at least in large part, by their faith. We see that in people such as John Lewis, who studied and earned a degree at American Baptist University in Nashville and then later became a member of Congress after gaining recognition for leadership in the civil rights movement.

In the days of apartheid in South Africa, Bishop Desmond Tutu stood alongside Nelson Mandela to battle oppression there and won the Nobel Peace Prize in 1984 in recognition of his efforts. Around the world, it is often people of faith who are at the forefront of movements for civil rights and basic freedoms.

The examples of these religious leaders in the battle to help the oppressed around them gives evidence to the moral benefit that religion can provide to society, and helps illustrate the secular case for religion.

Eleven

Summary

In each of the areas discussed above, the examples given are just that: examples. There are many more churches and synagogues and religious organizations that work in each of those areas and more. The examples mentioned serve their communities by reaching out to the poor, needy, sick and enslaved and there are more similar outreach groups in most every part of the country and these stories are duplicated numerous times and in numerous places.

The original challenge of this whole discussion was a question around charitable giving and what good, if any, was giving to churches, synagogues and other religious groups to people who were not religious.

Yet, as we have seen, there is a lot of good that churches and religious groups do for society and the people around them. There is a secular case for religion, a benefit from religion even for those who are not particularly religious.

And we have shown that is the case across a broad range of concerns and areas of need, and religious organizations reaching out in areas of need within the community has a long history.

Charitable giving to religion, meaning money given to churches, synagogues or other religious institutions is not solely used for religion (although people who are religious, and who give their money, would not necessarily object if it was). That money is used to express religious principles that include Judeo-Christian commands to help widows, orphans and others in need. For those who are religious and try to follow their religious principles, those religious and moral precepts are then reflected in their lives. As such, they are reflected in ways that benefit society and the world around them. And the more that they express their beliefs, the more there is a tangible benefit to people in need and to society, as a whole.

When religious people and organizations live out their faith by reaching out to those in need and to those who are oppressed, that isn't a strictly religious exercise. So even nonreligious people benefit from those who are religious living by their beliefs. Having people of faith, having churches, synagogues and faith-based organizations within a community helps that community to be a better and more caring place. Society and communities benefit from religion, even if they may care nothing about religion itself. To an objective observer, there can be little doubt that there is a secular case for religion.

Epilogue

The discussion has been about the benefits of religion even to people who may not be religious, about how there is a secular case for religion. Yet, to be objective, there would also be those that would argue that religion has brought bad things at times in history. And, candidly, there have been those times.

In the context of Christianity, the one that would probably be mentioned most often is the Crusades. The argument would be that religion was used as an excuse to commit violence to pursue conquest in a foreign land. However, the historiography of the Crusades has changed over time, and current scholarship does not see the Crusades as solely religious wars of forced conversion or conquest.

Yet even if the history of the Crusades is not quite as straightforward as some popular culture would portray, the point is still valid: that there are times that religion has been used to excuse bad things, including, at times, periods or events of terrible violence. The Spanish Inquisition and the conversion of native peoples in the Americas by threats of physical violence are two examples. We would have to admit that there are instances where religion has been used as an excuse for bad things, including in these cases torture and death. More recently, we could point to small but extremist cults like that of Jim Jones, who had his small group of followers commit mass suicide.

Theologians would point out that such things were not a reflection of Christian teaching or Biblical text. The actions of the people involved who committed crimes in the name of religion were not a reflection of the true teachings of that religion. Yet even if that is the case (and I certainly believe that it is), that doesn't change the fact that those things were done in the name of religion. Human institutions are also victims of human frailties and vanities and the more powerful those institutions are, the more likely they are to become corrupt. Even if that powerful institution is a church.

Looking at the broader context, the concern about religious violence even today is about religions who believe they are not only right but believe that being right allows them to use force and violence to convert others or to enforce their beliefs. Such would be the case in the terrorist attacks on 9/11 or the war by ISIS to set up a caliphate in the Middle East. These Islamic groups believe in jihad, holy wars that are justified in enforcing their religious beliefs upon others. In the world in which we live, that is a concern, in some places more than others.

That is not to minimize the instances in history, or places in the world today, where religion has been the excuse to do terrible things. Those things happened and exist and we can't deny it.

Yet, we also should not go the opposite extreme of those who are not just nonreligious but antireligious because of the massive evils they may suggest that come from religion. That is not the case either.

There is often pretty pointed hyperbole on that extreme, as well. There are those who would suggest that most wars in history have been caused by religion. A casual observer of history would readily realize that is not the case and really not even close. A review of wars through known history has estimated between roughly 7-11 percent of wars were for religious reasons.[6] So certainly there have been wars over religion but to suggest that a majority of the wars have a religious nature would be much more rhetoric than fact.

Honest reflection must admit that bad things have been done at times in the name of religion, and certainly religious people and institutions are not always pure and just. This epilogue is an acknowledgement of that valid point.

At the same time, that does not diminish the broader point made: society benefits from giving to religious charities. And those religious charities provide tangible, measureable benefit to the people and communities around them. Tens of billions of dollars a year are given to religious charities, a significant amount of which is passed on in the ways that we have talked about above. These groups, and the individuals that make up these groups, fill in gaps where the government cannot or isn't able. In filling those gaps, we all benefit and can be grateful. Because even for the most secular among us, there is a case for religion.

---

[6] For background see Holt, Andrew, "Counting Religious Wars in the Encyclopedia of Wars" apholt.com, accessed December 29, 2020 and Holt, Andrew, "Religion and the 100 Worst Atrocities in History" apholt.com, accessed December 29, 2020

Printed in the United States
by Baker & Taylor Publisher Services